© Copyright Elisabeth Cooper

All right reserved
Duplication in any form without written permission from the author is prohibited

ISBN: 979-8-9943032-3-8

Zion Volume One
Splendor

By Elisabeth Cooper

ZAHAV
PUBLISHING

Dedication

I want to dedicate this work to two people, without whom, I would not be the person I am. I have come through a great storm thriving because you have both held the truth of who I was created to be in the midst of devastation, and have stood unwavering in love and strength.

YANA SANDERS
אמא שלי

Your constant love is my anchor.
The expression and creative output of my life cannot be separated from the beauty of your love for me. Everything I create has threads of your love woven woven throughout, shining brilliantly in strength, purity, and light. This book exists, in large part, because of
Your unfailing belief in who I am.

REBECCA COOPER

My sister, my best friend.
You are the most faithful person I know.
Always straight as an arrow, never wavering in truth and justice. You have stood with me in everything; always speaking in honesty and strength.
The gift of you in my life is one of the reasons I have weathered the storms as well as I have. Your beauty and depth inspire me continually.

Forward

By Dr. Yana Sanders

Welcome to a life altering inward encounter with Zion. These words convey YHVH'S heart for His chosen dwelling place on earth! Elisabeth Cooper has carefully crafted elegant words raging with frequency to convey an aspect of YHVH'S heart that has not been shared until now! Each page, paragraph, and sentence is an epic journey. She is indeed a modern day classic poet who carries the heart and breath of Zion.

Elisabeth's entanglement with Zion and her depth of relationship with The Lord have opened an ancient pathway. She intentionally carries us beyond present day religious constructs and dogmas. Her exquisite use of words brings us into alignment with YHVH'S heart. Courageously, she invites us into an intimate connection from within the voice, frequency, and heart of Zion. As a result, a powerful visceral shift occurs in our understanding of the chosen dwelling place of YHVH.

Through both complex and multilayered words, Elisabeth guides her audience into a realm of heaven few have known or understood. This evokes images infused with powerful feelings that penetrate the boundaries of our hearts going deeper than any language. Every poem is a pool of living waters; healing, cleansing, and awakening. Calling to the deep parts of our hearts yearning to live. Through a dynamic inward journey these poems call our hearts to "prepare the way of the LORD " for His return to Zion. This is who Elisabeth Cooper is- it is what she does. She intimately *knows* the heart of Zion, and is a tender, compassionate protector of truth. She is an ancient soul connected at a cellular level to the call of YHVH for our "Return to Zion".

To know and understand Zion is to know the *Lord of Zion*. She skillfully cuts away the layers of religious rhetoric and brings Zion into a current focus from the ancient path. May you be washed in the healing waters of these words. May the LORD of Zion - the 3 in one - call you deeper. For it is written, " The time to favor Zion has come..."

What an exquisite, dynamic, life impacting gift Elisabeth has given. Spoken words do not tell the full story of what transpires deep within the quiet places of our hearts. Take your time with each poem, be present and allow a fresh breath of life to revive and strengthen you. Let the healing waters call you into alignment with YHVH and Zion- His chosen dwelling place within you.

Dr. Yana Sanders

Introduction

When I set out to write this book, my life looked different than it does today. In the past few years I have been through some storms I didn't see coming. The book got delayed. It is precisely because of those storms, and that delay, that this book that you now hold became what it is. The initial vision for the book remained, but the content grew deeper. Perhaps one of the greatest truths I have known throughout my life is that the Father is near to the brokenhearted. I have lived that reality through these storms. I have known immeasurable comfort, beauty, goodness, and truth as I have walked with the King of the Universe through challenges I wasn't sure I could face. Because of this, my heart and life expanded to hold treasures untold. Some of those treasures will remain untold, kept in the sacred space of holy friendship.

My friendship with heaven means everything to me. I would trade everything for it. In many ways, I have. And so, the book you hold in your hands contains more than poetry and prose with a few essays sprinkled in. It contains a life poured out in devotion to all of heaven. It contains the sound on the trading floor for the heartbeat of Zion.

My deepest desire for you as you read the words on the following pages, is that you would see just a glimmer of the splendor of Zion worth all our lives could offer, that fire and truth would spark in your heart of the extraordinary life you were created to live in this era and the age to come, that you would truly come to know and understand that you were created uniquely for this time to walk as a king and a priest in the order of Melchizedek, and that saying yes to all of this is worth it all.

The majority of this book was written in Israel. That was incredibly intentional. I wanted the heart of Zion, both heavenly Zion and Zion on earth, to resound in every utterance of these words. It was written over the course of several years during my times in Israel. Listen, you can hear the sound of Zion. Close your eyes between the words and see beyond what you've known. Breathe deeper the air you were created to breathe, the air of the eternal city of light.

As I have done with this introduction, I will continue with a personal tone that is more on the informal side in the pieces of writing at the beginning of each section of poetry. This is intentional. I am choosing to sit with you and speak like a friend from my heart and less like a lecturing teacher. So, let's sit together in the Light of Zion and let Wisdom and Goodness lead us.

Listen.
Zion is singing.
Let's dance.

Contents

Aleph   1   *Zion Shining : Splendor*   א

Bet   2   *HaAretz (The Land)*   ב

Gimel   3   *Zion Culture*   ג

Dalet   4   *Zion People*   ד

Hey   5   *Priesthood of Zion*   ה

And now, friends...

Have the courage
To walk away
From falsity

Even when
It's all you've
Ever known

Gather your strength
To see the talons
Of systems
Built to be prisons

They were
Not invented
For the good
Of your heart

Truth
Holds
Real
Life

It's time to come home
Zion is calling

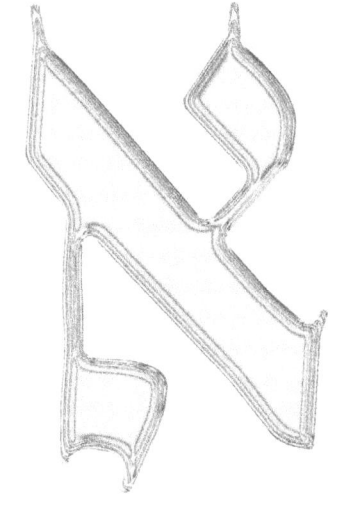

Zion Shining
Splendor

1

ZION VOLUME ONE : SPLENDOR

Zion Shining: Splendor

Ever since I was a young, I was fascinated by Zion. I loved the scriptures about Zion. I would read them over and over and dream of Zion. As a kid, I didn't have very much head knowledge about Zion, nor did very many people talk about it. So, I spent my life engaging with Zion in my heart with the Lord and all of heaven. I explored, setting my heart to understand, and most of all, being in enraptured by heavenly Zion. Constantly drawn to Zion on earth. We must understand that both exist, both are true, and both have a purpose. To accept one while denying the other is to walk half-blinded to the fullness of Yahweh's heart and plans.

As above, so below (more commonly stated- on earth as it is in heaven), is far more than a good prayer. It is the dream, blueprint, and reality of the heart of Yahweh from the beginning.

"In the beginning Elohim created the heavens and the earth..." This is the common English translation of Genesis 1:1. But in order to know the truth, we must let the Hebrew tell the story.

We barely have to scratch the surface of the Hebrew here to see powerful truth.

The phrase we will focus on here is "heavens and the earth".

Hashamayim v'et Ha'aretz

Hashamayim: Translated the heavens. The direct translation is the waters, which informs us of the atmosphere of heaven.

V'et- directly translated "and the". Et is a word which translators will tell you doesn't have a translation. They say it is the sign of the direct object. But there's something much deeper to this word. Et is spelled Aleph Tav. Aleph being the first letter of the Aleph Bet, and Tav being the last letter of the Aleph Bet. Who is the beginning and the end? You may know the title as the "Alpha and Omega". But Yeshua wasn't Greek. He didn't speak Greek. He was Jewish, and He spoke Hebrew. He is the beginning and the end and everything in between. He is the Aleph and the Tav. And that Hebrew letter vav right before Et? We'll talk about that in a minute.

Ha'Aretz: is commonly translated "the earth". The direct translation of the Hebrew is "The Land". Furthermore, Aretz has always been the nickname for Israel. When you say Ha'aretz in Israel, it will be interpreted as Israel. Aretz refers to Israel, the literal land of Israel.

If we gather all this together we see something incredibly beautiful and powerful:

We see that in the beginning Elohim created the heavens/the waters above (hashamayim) and the (v'et: again, directly translated and Yeshua) the land of Israel (ha'aretz).

Why is this important? Because in the very first utterance of Torah, the whole entire story is told. The blueprint of His heart is laid out for us.

We know that there is a heavenly Zion (as above)
We know that Yeshua was slain before the foundations of the world were laid.

Yeshua, who was, and is, and is to come, was there from before the foundations of the earth were laid, slain; with nails in his hands and feet...He is the Aleph and the Tav that sits between Hashamayim (The heavens/waters) and Ha'aretz (The Land-Israel). And that Hebrew letter Vav joined to the Aleph and the

Tav? That Vav is holding worlds together. The world of Hashamayim and the world of Ha'aretz. You see, the letter Vav in the ancient pictorial language of Hebrew is a nail, the connector, the stake in the ground, the fastener. It acts as a connector in its function within the Hebrew language as well. To add Vav to the beginning of a word, is to add "and". The great connector of words, thoughts, truths.

And as there is a heavenly Zion, a holy city, a New Jerusalem. There is an earthly Zion, a holy city, an earthly Jerusalem. From the very beginning, there's been a quantum fastener: Yeshua.

And as He was slain before the foundations of the earth were laid (It's always been complete), but He also needed to come in physical form to the earth and give his life as the Lamb slain; so, too, is the New Jerusalem complete and fully existing, but also must come down in physical form to the earth.

What I see happening in the earth now is what I call the resonant frequency of Zion. "The time to favor Zion has come." When one tuning fork with a similar makeup to another gets struck and is brought near an un-struck tuning fork of the same frequency, the un-struck tuning fork begins to hum with the very same song. When more than one body of frequency begins to hum with the same frequency as another, science calls this a resonant system.

The songs, the frequency, the ways, the truth and beauty of Zion is ringing out, and those with the same frequency are beginning to hum with the same song. There is a resonant frequency of Zion building in the earth, and it will continue to build until heavenly Zion and the New Jerusalem have a physical fusion with earthly Zion and earthly Jerusalem.

This resonant frequency sounds like:

> A priesthood of a new order rising with clean hands and a pure heart.

An awakening to the ancient paths and the eternal ways of Zion.

The rhythm of the eternal feasts of Yahweh in the earth as it is in heaven.

And so until that great day when this resonant frequency manifests into a complete fusion in the natural, we sing with our entire beings the songs of Zion!

ZION VOLUME ONE : SPLENDOR

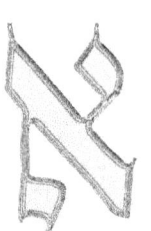

Atmosphere

Air and water
dance together
in singular blue
in sapphire brightness

Clear and high
the light is alive
in opalescent fire

The sound at once
soothes and wakes
The temple garden
sings

Song
Water
Color
Light

Lives
in every inhale
of mountain air

The tangibility
of the living
atmosphere
of Zion

Crystal Cave

Take a deep breathe

Close your eyes

Feel the quiet

Breathe

Imagine
a Crystal Cave
river waters
up to the banks

The walls
all
made
of crystals

A small rowboat
carries you
into the depths
of the gems of
The New Jerusalem

These gems
wait
for their song
to resound
in hearts

For that song
to travel
from hearts
into hands

And as those hands
reach to touch

They begin
to breathe
on earth
And
sing
the songs
of
Zion

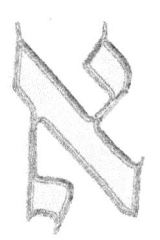

Zion

Zion
At once in heaven
and on earth

And from the time
the Lamb
was slain
He held
the reality
of the fusion
of Zion
in His heart

Before the land
breathed
Him in
it was destined
to hold the city
of gold and precious stones
and the light of the Lamb
forever

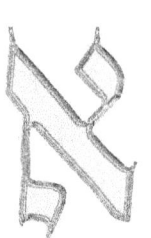

Emerald Air

The Highest place I could live
is the lowest place I could bow

Breathing clearest atmosphere

Shimmering waters
through my lungs

I take in
the emerald air
of mercy and justice

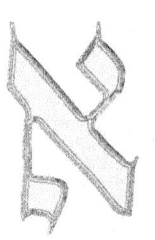

Leaves and Angels

Leaves fall
to the sound
of angels dancing
in the symphony
that plays
inside the quiet refrain
of stillness
in the center
of a wheel
within a wheel

The universe
breathes The Name
in spheres and rhythms
unbroken

אל עולם

El Olam - God Everlasting/of the Universe

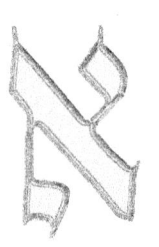

Songs of Zion

The wind knows me
I sing to it
songs of Zion
and breaking dawn

When it answers
it delivers in its breath
every comfort
of magnificent
redemption

Within currents
In movement
upon waters
In the kiss
upon the trees
it tells of ancient wisdom

And as I sing
to the wind
The wind sings
to me

The four winds
bend their ear towards
this symphonic friendship
with a humble priest
born to speak the tongue
of Love

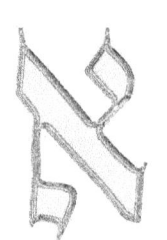

Seeds

When the seeds of tomorrow
start speaking today

Listen

Favor rests on the song
that pulls up the sun

When ancient eternal melodies
surge into this moment

Attune

They're here to create
Zion's reality

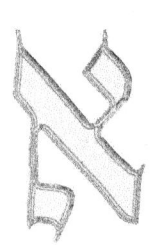

Poetry Beyond Words

Zion speaks louder
Exceeding words

We walk with holy
living ones

They rarely speak in human language
but we are taught

Zion teaches
in living letters
in holy colors
in music
and poetry

In light
beyond all
this world confines

Enveloped
in heart language
We come alive
to truth and wisdom

We are taught

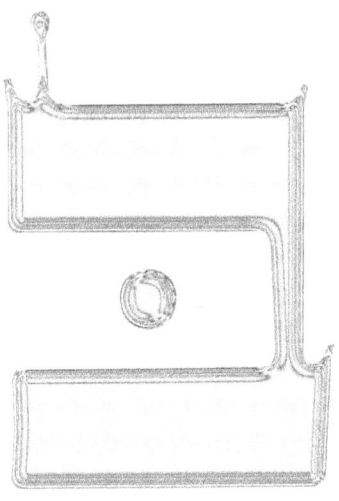

HaAretz
The Land

2

ZION VOLUME ONE : SPLENDOR

HaAretz: The Land

There is nothing like being in the land of Israel. The eternal nature of the very ground the sole of one's foot touches with every step is undeniable. It speaks of ages and generations past, present, future. It leads into the very splendor of heavenly Zion. It's all there. Deep truth speaks from the land.

If we will let it in, we will see not just new and ancient cities we can learn great and beautiful things from, but the very living, breathing heartbeat of the King of Zion. Walking in Israel with an open and listening heart will change your life forever. As I've walked in the land, I have felt the Ancient and Eternal, the very present and distinct heartbeat of Yahweh. The frequency of the land speaks.

In these poems, I have captured a minute portion of what I have heard, and what I experience in the land I now consider a friend. As you read them (even if you've never walked in Israel), open up to a new reality of the ancient, the new, the eternal voice of the land of Zion singing, teaching, listening. Let these words take you on a journey, knowing that the land of Israel sings the songs of heavenly Zion. Grab a cup of coffee (Turkish if you really want to feel like you're in Israel), open your heart, sit with the Land for a while, feel its wonders, hear its voice.

The Land

To sit with the land
is to learn its song

Listen closely and you'll hear
the song of before

And maybe you can help sing it back
in forgotten places

And maybe it will remind your ancient soul
how to sing

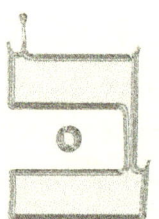

Galilee

The voice of the birds
holds close the waters
Immense
Robust
and altogether captivating

A dawn song that will
wake your being
to know the fiery sunrise
wrapped in the glory of morning

An afternoon melody that
exhales strength and sweetness
A song of sustained perpetuity

The masterpiece of dusk
that sings the sun and moon
into their glorious exchange

This birdsong wields
A specificity of life
Comfort
Strength
Courage
Joy

The birds here
herald the song
of the water
In enduring faithfulness
they sing:

Surety and peace
Power and completion

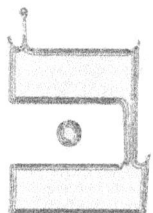

Tel Aviv

There are schisms of light
in chaos
chinks in the armor
of what seems
altogether
consumed
by unrelenting pressure

Stillness and quiet
breathe
amidst heartache
there is a silence
so cavernous
you can find yourself

Survival's wrestle
is not always
a brawl
but the steady calm
of a face set like flint

And in all of this
the light settles
into the morning
and we find
someone has fed
the birds

Yafo (Jaffa)

I love the old port city of Yaffo. I have spent many an evening while in Israel standing at the water's edge there; engaging the waters (Mem) of that ancient and important place. One of the most recognizable portions of that history being that it was the port that Yonah (Jonah) set sail from. And on one particular evening, I had the most beautiful encounter with Yonah and with the waters of that port city. It brought my heart into a deeper place of understanding, and helped me move forward in my own life. I know the truth about Yonah will touch your heart as well.

Yonah is often depicted as a grumpy, disobedient, whiny baby, running from God. But I want to help us reframe that a bit.

Several years ago I listened as Dr. Yana Sanders opened up some deeply important truths about the life of Yonah. What we don't realize in the modern retelling of His story in the western church is how incredible Yonah was, the anguish he suffered, and exactly why he didn't want to go to Nineveh. You wouldn't either, if you were Yonah, trust me. He wasn't petty. He wasn't just a whiny punk who disobeyed God. Yonah was a man who was given the opportunity to forgive and bring the redemption of the heart of the Lord to a people who had absolutely devastated his life personally.

The Ninevites were not just some random people that Yonah didn't care for. The Ninevites destroyed Yonah's young life and killed his entire family right in front of him in the most brutal and unimaginable ways. That is why Yonah didn't want to go to Nineveh. I'm not sure I'd want to go to Nineveh after seeing the Ninevites rape, torture, and kill my mother and sisters; after seeing them torture and kill and chop my family into pieces. I might not want to go to Nineveh.

Can you imagine the flood of emotional trauma and triggers (to say the least) that the thought of going to Nineveh would cause Yonah? Not to mention the fear. I imagine seeing these barbarians at their worst as a young boy, would cause Yonah some concern, to put it lightly.

So, you see, there's more to Yonah's story than we've known. There's far a more to Yonah than we have perceived. And Yonah deserves far more honor than he's been given. I think Yonah shows us an incredible picture of a man whom the Lord saw fit to rise to an unthinkable occasion, a man that the Lord believed in, a man who understandably wrestled, but who ultimately went to Nineveh and delivered the heart of the Lord to the very people who tortured and killed his entire family right in front of him. A man who was spared as a child, but left to deal with unimaginable horrors, loss, and grief. When we hear the truth about Yonah's story, when we see the humanity of Yonah and what he overcame, we can begin to have compassion and honor for a man who worked through insurmountable trauma, and successfully poured the heart of the Lord to the last people on earth he wanted to do that for.

There's so much to say about Yonah. He is incredible. This particular night at the water's edge, as I encountered his heart, connected with the land, and engaged with Mem in the form of the Mediterranean Sea, I saw how Yonah encountered Mem; how he sought temporary comfort and a hiding place within Mem, but instead Mem delivered him into the hands of truth and the rough tumbling ground of healing and forgiveness. Sometimes our path to emotional wellness and forgiveness can be just that, a rough tumbling ground.

I am comforted in this- the God of the Universe knows and sees exactly what our hearts need to bring us into our utmost and ultimate destiny. We can trust Him, all of heaven, and the entire universe He created fully.

Thank you, Yonah, for your incredible life, and for cheering us on from the great cloud of witnesses unto the fulfillment of our ultimate potential; For cheering us on right alongside those repentant Ninevites, who you now call friends.

ZION VOLUME ONE : SPLENDOR

Jerusalem

To hold all you've held
To see all you've seen
And still grip tightly
to truth
Enduring light
Holy City

Pressure surrounds you
Chaos swirls within

But in the midst
beats
your heart
in stillness dancing

You carry the weight
with grace

The tears of generations
You hold
with a Mother's arms

A brilliant beacon
of beauty
Jerusalem of Gold

Eternal celebration
resounds within your gates

And in your great holding
Held is the promise
Born is
The day of His appearing

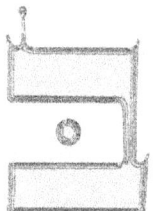

Caesarea

When the rhythm
of this water holds you
The arms of Clarity and Constance
bear you up

Tumbled in clear intention

If you move with water
If you trust it
The landscape
of you
will change
with every wave

For the stones
that have seen atrocity
Washed and tumbled
by water and time
Will soon bear witness
of the power of the waters
To make smooth the jagged edges
unto holy

Mikvah waters live
to make alive

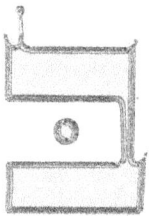

Kaphar Nachum (Capernum)

The Ancient Way of Comfort
Is the abounding way of Zion

To be held
Surrounded
Kept warm

To be fed
Nurtured
Gently taught

Is empowerment unto greatness

The ancient way of comfort
Is the strength of the warrior
From the heights of Zion

As scrolls unroll
And we walk the words
Of the ancient path
Into the light of a new dawn
Arms of comfort hold us
softness strengthens us
And we are not afraid

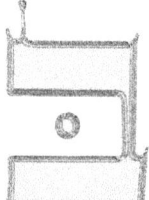

The Sea of Salt (Dead Sea)

You may not perceive
Conventional life
Here

But salt grows softness
If you let it
And depth grows quiet

Wild heat
Presses fragrance
From desert blooms

Dawn is breaking

Breath is in the river

And I can feel
Fresh water's current
Rising
Over my feet

All the priests
And kings
Stand up
And sing
The song
Of Zion

חזיה

chayah- live, be alive, revive, sustaining life, restoring to life

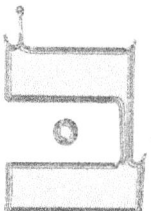

Abraham's Gate

Stones remember
Gates remain
Daughters and sons stand
Listening
Living
to sing
the new and everlasting songs
of holiness and light
We are the gates
Standing in the gate

Ein Gedi

The caves and waters
Still speak
Of a tender-hearted
Shepherd warrior
Who let a righteous heart
Bellow full voiced
In the face of Saul's
Unrelenting
Pursuit to destroy
Destiny

The frequency of
Of standing up
In righteousness
And identity
Pours from that cave
Like the waters below it
Pour in a fall
Into clear fresh pool

If you listen, you can hear
David standing up
Into all his heart knew he was-
A king and a priest
Of an entirely different order

On that day
The shepherd
Became a King
Who was a priest
Who was a shepherd
Who was a witness in the earth
Of a priesthood rising
For the glory of Zion

Cavernous rocks
Fresh desert water
Still hold memory
And when true
Kings and priests
Stand before that cave
Under those waters
The whole universe
Crescendos with them
For a priesthood
Standing

The Kotel

Even the Sparrows Have Found a Home?

Years ago I was reading about swifts (small birds) at the Kotel (Western Wall). It turns out the Kotel is one of the oldest swift nesting sites in the world. These incredible birds have been nesting at the Kotel for longer than 2,000 years. Israel, as a whole, is one of the busiest avian migratory junctions in the world for birds of all kinds. The morning dawn song just before sunrise is one of the most breathtaking I've ever experienced, especially in Jerusalem and Galilee. I've done a lot of world travel, but the birds in Israel are something special. Their song, in symphony with the land, produces a frequency so singular in its beauty and clarity, you come that much closer to understanding their "words" completely.

Swifts are unique because they spend their years predominantly in the air. They live most of their life in the air; eating, drinking, mating, even sleeping in the air! They only land to nest and lay eggs.

Why is this significant?

As I read multiple articles about the Swifts at the Kotel, that scripture in Psalms 84 came to my mind:

> *"Even the sparrow has found a home, and the swallow a nest for herself, where she may lay her young, at your altars, O Lord of Hosts, my King and my God."*

I love this scripture, but I decided to do some study into it because I had a feeling this common English translation had, once again, removed us from the story that the Hebrew tells, and separated us from the true meaning and beauty. As I did a little study of the Hebrew, I discovered that was, indeed, the case. It isn't the *sparrow* has found a home. It's the swift.

What's the difference?

Sparrows are perching birds. It is not difficult for them to find a home, for them to be perched on the earth. They nest everywhere. They land everywhere. They spend a good amount of time anchored, if you will, to the earth.

As I mentioned above, swifts live predominantly in the air. They do not anchor to the earth. They live their lives in the realm of the air, and are more acclimated to the air than they are to the earth. They do not easily find, or want, a permanent home in the earth.

So, to say that even the sparrow has found a home is nothing remarkable or meaningful. But to say that even the swift has found a home is something deep and meaningful. I do believe that the Psalmist was specifically talking about the walls of the temple in this Psalm. If we look at the entirety of the Psalm, it is a Psalm about the temple, the courts of the Lord, the altar and the house of the Lord.

One changed word in translation changes the entirety of meaning. The implication and application for the truth of what it *actually* says has been powerful for me personally. I feel like the swift much of the time; more oriented to the air than I am anchored to the earth. Maybe you resonate with that. In the grand scheme of things, we are all made to be in the world not of it, and to set our whole being on things above, to live in the high places, but to still find a place of home, to still be in this world. We deeply need a place of home and safety, a touch point that anchors us for the purpose of fruitfulness in the earth. A place we can be grounded for the sake of Zion in the earth. Our wings must always fly in the heights and realms, but our feet must know a solid place in the earth; that we would be the dwellers of another world, but that we would also be the ones who bring those two worlds together. The dwellers of mystery who walk the earth breathing the frequency of awe into the sleeping. The dwellers of the reality of the King of Zion and His holy city, who touch the earth and the hearts of the people with light and love absolute, which brings justice and makes all things new.

In this whole world, in all my travels, I have found very few places that feel like home. The first time I came to the Kotel, I felt like my heart had found a grounding place in this earth. The Kotel is singular in the earth, unmatched in what it has seen and continues to carry. Matter has memory and those stones hold the laughter and tears of the ancients and generations upon generations of communion with Yahweh in that place. The frequency there is like none other in any other place on the earth, and creation bears witness. The swifts, who love the air more than they love the land, have spoken with their choice to find a home there for generations. To choose that place is to make a statement to earth and to show us as we return home, what it looks like to hold worlds together underneath these skies.

When you visit The Kotel during their 3 month stay to nest at the Kotel, you will experience one of the most astonishing things. These remarkable birds fly speedily in circles overhead day and night, and as the songs and prayers crescendo, listen to the swifts, they raise their song in tandem.

ZION VOLUME ONE : SPLENDOR

"How lovely is your dwelling place, O Lord of Hosts! My soul longs, yes, even faints for the courts of the Lord; my heart and flesh sing for joy to the living God. Even the swift finds a home, and the swallow a nest for herself, where she may lay her young, at your altars, O Lord of Hosts, my King and my God. Blessed are those who dwell in your house, ever singing your praise! Blessed are those whose strength is in You, in whose heart are the highways of Zion."

Psalm 84: 2-6

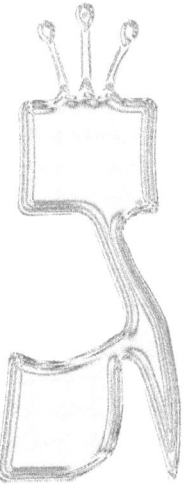

Zion Culture

3

ZION VOLUME ONE : SPLENDOR

Zion Culture

"...'Come let us go up to the mountain of the Lord, to the house of the God of Jacob; that He may teach us concerning His ways and that we may walk in His paths.' For the Law will go forth from Zion, and the word of the Lord from Jerusalem." Isaiah 2:3

As we talk about the culture of Zion here, I want to say first and foremost, the important thing is not first what you *do*, but who you *are*! That is the way of Zion. Zion is outside man-made systems, Babylonian systems, man-made religion. In our relationship with Zion we connect with the government that rests on His shoulders, His heart, and ways. That government is a government of relationship, purity, truth, beauty, and justice.

Zion is singular in holy culture. The culture of Zion is counter to most everything western culture lauds and celebrates. I have long said that the ways and weapons of Zion are unassuming, but they win. Rest, beauty, joy, covenant, nurturing, etc. When we think of realities like rest and beauty, they are not things our culture typically credits power to, yet the power and victory of Zion sits squarely in that which seems powerless.

When you live in the ways of Zion, most of the world will not understand you, but you will thrive. For me, personally, the systems of the world and man-made religion are completely upside down to me. They are so contrary to the ways of The Lord, the ways of Zion. Zion is completely relational. There is no pattern or way of doing anything in Zion outside of relationship. This alone disqualifies most systems of the world and man-made religion should they ever claim to be a reflection of the heart of Yahweh. If it is more transactional than relational, it is not rooted in the ways of Zion.

I want nothing outside of the heart and ways of Zion in my life. I will follow no other path than the path of Zion. I was born in Zion, and in Zion I'll remain.

Drink deeply of the ancient well of Zion in these words and let your heart come alive. Remember where you were born and return home singing "All my springs of joy are in you."

His foundation is in the holy mountains.
*   The Lord loves the gates of Zion*
*   More than all the other dwelling places of Jacob.*
Glorious things are spoken of you,
*   O city of God.*
"I shall mention Rahab and Babylon among
*   those who know Me;*
Behold, Philistia and Tyre with Ethiopia.
*   'This one was born there.' "*
But of Zion it shall be said, "This one and
*   that one were born in her";*
And the Most High Himself will establish her.
The Lord will count when He registers the peoples,
*   "This one was born there."*
Then whose who sing as well as those who
*   play the flutes shall say,*
"All my springs of joy are in you."

Psalm 87:1-7

ZION VOLUME ONE : SPLENDOR

Rest

Time bends
For rest
And lungs
Stretch
To fit
The breadth
Of an entire
Universe
Of song
And light

Rest
Is higher
Truth
With a
Voice
Bigger
Than
The illusion
Of time

To sit
In what is
Complete
To trust
In what is
Finished
To know
What is
True

Is to live
In
The victory
Of rest

Faithfulness

Faithfulness
is its own kind
of Quantum catapult

Faithfulness
in choosing joy
is its own
limitless
life

Choose joy
and you choose
Life

Choose joy
and you breathe
into
the life
you want
to live

Let joy
crown
your heart
with golden
abundance

Walk free

The Way of Prayer

My prayer shines with
Less words
More heart language
Less conscious
And more connection
Lacking the taste of
One tree
Growing the fruit
Of life

The Language of Zion

From the breath of angels
The void of darkness
The illuminated song of God

Poetry creates

From beauty, from pain
From colors unseen
From hidden light

Poetry creates

From paths of Zion
A new city shines
Spoken, sung, and played on strings

Poetry creates

And the letters that live rejoice

שירה יצר

Shirah Yotzer - Poetry/Song/Singing creates

Counterfeit

Looking for what glitters
Instead of what's gold
Is the way of folly
That leads to counterfeit

Let your heart know Zion
Gold eternal
Rejecting the imposter
Shimmering
With dark enticement

For it will rise
To lure hearts
But those who's hearts
know Zion
Will remain unmoved
From the incorruptible
Mountain

Gold

Illuminated

Rest

Come back home
to the kind of softness
that stands separate
from the fury
of the world's
systems and storms

Return again
to the stillness
which accelerates
every moment
into forward motion
beyond constraint
and limits

Rest

Zion reverberates
unmatched
in all power
and goodness
because
Rest
is the fabric
of its movement

Counterfeits

Where there is reality, there will always be a truth-less, holographic image void of heavenly substance rising up to usurp the name of true identity. Simply put, where the real exists, there will always be a counterfeit. Zion is no exception. The priesthood of Zion (The order of Melchizedek) is no exception.

You can spot a counterfeit a mile away if you are tuned into, and resonating with, the real. When it comes to Zion, and the order of Melchizedek, it's fairly simple. If you need complicated codes, formulas, and mental ascent; if it's run by rote systems and algorithms void of the thundering voice of Elohim charged with every Hebrew living letter which comprises all creation, you're probably looking at a counterfeit. If it operates outside of honest and authentic relationship, you're looking at a counterfeit. The counterfeits sound brilliant, captivate with promising power, and negate pillars of truth while creating their own culture of ascent. Babylonian-esq shine and frequency, which only those born in Zion will ascertain as counterfeit.

While heavenly Zion is a city of utmost order, brilliance, and efficiency, it is without the constraints of formula and rote systems. While the Priesthood of Zion is clear and noble and drips with abundance in every way, it is without arrogance or feigned power. Everything about Zion is pure, upheld, directed, and created by the power of the heart.

While Yahweh creates in brilliant and powerful patterns and designs, they do not depart from wild breath and fire, from the untethered way of water, from freedom, from *life*. They are patterns that breathe. They are constructs of creation that move with every heartbeat of heaven. Babylon builds impressive structures, but they are void of the power of truth and the breath of life.

The efficiency and brilliance lies in its values, its heart, in relationship. There is a relationship of heart connect between every element of Zion and those who dwell in it. Everything is seen and valued and known beyond formula and function. Values in Zion seem upside down from values of earth. These values certainly don't commune with power-seeking, system creating, formula loving hearts who will not yield their limited understanding in order to know the power and unmatched ability of clean hands and a pure heart to lead the way in every eternal way of Zion.

Put Zion in your eyes, attune your ears to the frequency of Zion, fill your heart with awakening to the ways of Zion. It is only then that the counterfeits will crumble and Babylon will lose its hold on hearts longing for the true and pure.

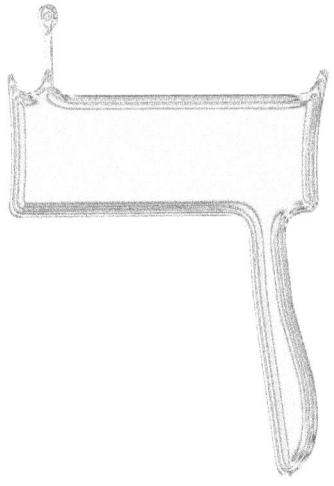

Zion People

4

ZION VOLUME ONE : SPLENDOR

Zion People

I first bellowed out the phrase "Zion People" many years ago in the middle of a worship set I was leading. In the middle of this glorious spontaneous worship session, I saw a vision of people of light coming up out of the earth everywhere. They were a new, but ancient breed. They were different than anything the earth had seen.

I began to sing what I was seeing about these people:

They didn't care for man-made religious systems or what anyone thought of them. They cared only for, and followed only the ways of the heart of Yahweh. They didn't make a new system or a new religion, they simply lived biblical lives with all their hearts. The things I saw these people of light doing were astounding, but even more astounding were their hearts, their surety in their identity. They were immovable in truth, unstoppable.

After I described what I saw, I then sang "Who are these people?" a few times over. The intensity in the room was electric and building more and more, and then I heard myself bellow "These are the Zion people!" The room exploded. I will never forget it. It was a moment that shifted hearts and split the atmosphere. It truly felt like something was born into the the earth that night. I know for a fact a new understanding was birthed in my heart that would further fuel my life-long love of Zion. That moment would serve to bring me into an understanding of my destiny beyond words.

Zion and Zion People became a more prominent message of my life. I continually study, but more importantly, I live it. That's one thing about the Zion people; they're less about talk and more about action. Talk means nothing if you aren't authentic. Zion people live the power of being! Zion people don't need to tell of their greatness. They live in the delight of all of heaven, and they are convinced of who they are. They choose the power of *being* over the temporal praises and accolades of humanity for their deeds.

Zion people care only about following the ways of Yahweh, and will reject constructs that have nothing to do with His heart and ways.

Zion people love His eternal feasts.

Zion people will leave everything and lose everything to stand in truth.

The poems in this chapter are reflections and truths from the journey of one who lives for Zion. You may find some of your own journey in them. Shining here, are words that call like a trumpet to higher level living, to a new and ancient way. Whispering here are words to comfort those who have walked a difficult road to live contrary to the systems of man. Finally, you will glimpse the Zion people, if only for a moment, but that moment could change your life forever.

Zion People and Storms

We worry about defeat
when the strong storm comes
So we stubborn our feet
into what we think we know
And we fasten our hearts
to systems we think secure

But the storm doesn't regard
frameworks we've built
And it will take to task
all our folly
in its wreckage

What few know
about surviving storms
is that the might lies
not in being unmovable
against the tempest tide
But in being the strength
that rises with every
violent wave

Resolute but fluid
ever knowing
the beauty
of surety
Ever building
with incorruptible
Truth

אֵל סַלְעִי

El Saliy - God my Rock/My strength/my stronghold

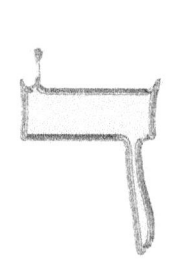

Valleys, deserts and ruin

Deep valleys
Lonely deserts
Dark clouds
Cities of ruin

I've seen them all
I've lived in some

Those who avoid valleys
never come to find the life
at the bottom

Those who are afraid of shadows
haven't realized the light
behind them

Those who trample ruins
haven't known the treasures
of brokenness

And those who fear the storm
have not known
what I have come to find

אדוני שמה

Adonai Shamah - My God is there

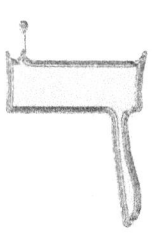

Untitled

Willful ignorance
of unworthy obstacles
is a gift to the righteous

Who never tire
in forever finding

Who always stand
lifting banners of victory

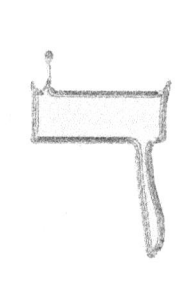

Overcomer's Road

I have walked the overcomer's road
Grace and pain
Beauty and crushing

I have known the hand of God
Resting heavy and gentle
Consistent and pure

I have known the tender softness of the world
And the rough tumbling ground
Where we become smooth

I walk the path of the ancients
I run on the highway of holiness
I sit in the flame of wisdom

And the alchemy of sorrow and joy
Sings the song of victory everlasting
In the constancy of loving kindness

אַתָּה גִּבּוֹר לְעוֹלָם אֲדֹנָי מְחַיֵּה מֵתִים אַתָּה

Atah Gibor Le'Olam Adonai Mehchaiyeh Mehtiym Atah

You are mighty, eternally, my Lord the Reviver of the dead, You are

Paradox

See how I hold close
Two
Seemingly opposing
Realities

Neither break
They are not torn
And I am not divided

Both unite
In the place of truth
And the hidden paths
Of wisdom

They are two walls
Of the same house
And contained
In their frame
Wholeness and fruit

Eyes that perceive
Are given to the seeker
Ever understanding

Only the wise
Find peace
In paradox

Only the righteous
Live forever
planted
By eternal streams

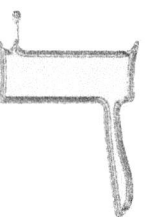

Endless Sparks

There is fire and light
the spectrum of God
in every
infinitesimal particle
created
yet to be created
seen and unseen

We get to breathe it in
We have been bestowed
with becoming
We are awakened to be
His walking fire,
light,
full spectrum

There is light we've not yet perceived
Colors we've not observed

But we are about to

We are about to become them

Endless sparks of the infinite

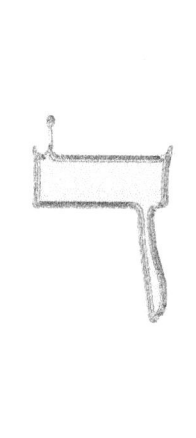

Sons and Daughters

We walked miles upon miles
Knowing and hoping
Singing songs that lit up the dark

We woke our bones
We pulled threads of lies
From the fabric of our hearts

To see clearly the form
To know deeply the divine

And here we are
Waking the earth

Coming Home

Before I became afraid
I was free

I was one
with the water and waves

I was friends
with fire

I ran into
the wind

My breath
was limitless

And I am coming home
to before

To the waters
of my making

Friendship and honor

Trepid waters
gather to harmonize
at the hands
of peace
they know

Hands of friendship
sweeping
over
chaotic
madness
to create beauty

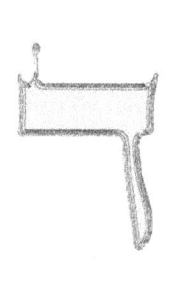

Rhythmic Reminder

I am a rhythmic reminder
to the earth

of origins
long forgotten

of ancient wells
covered over

of garden air
that sings of light

releasing remembrance
in enduring breath

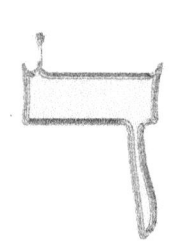

All I am

I don't yet comprehend
all I am
but I know it completely

My heart beats
with the fire
of Zion

In my veins
ladders spiral
and I'm not contained

I am not defined
by a system
or framework

I am outside time
A holy sacred
river

I run with horses
wild, unencumbered
And trample thickets
crossing over

Graceful Middle

In the graceful middle
of spinning chariots
and purposeful winds

I find myself
loosed
from the angry
prison masters
of my soul

And then
regathered
reclaimed
I walk
from the fierce waters and winds
to understand now
that I am the waters and winds
who rush the gates
and sing
of the breaking dawn

Remember : א

Deep
in the cavernous
eternity of your heart

The songs of Zion
Ring

Remember

Before the clamor
of society
and constructs
of Babylon
rose with piercing
peals

You were whole
in the river and rhythms
of Zion singing

Remember

Before every other voice
told you
who you were
and who you were not

You were complete
in the softness and strength
of the First Voice

Listen
Remember

Return

Remember what it feels like
to reside in peace and wholeness

Recall the grandeur
of your origins
You
Shimmering delight
of His heart

Breathe again
the song you were born in
on the heights of Zion, great
sounding
in magnificent power
Donned with the weight of glory

Return to the immovable Life
in you
The King's mountain tower
of truth

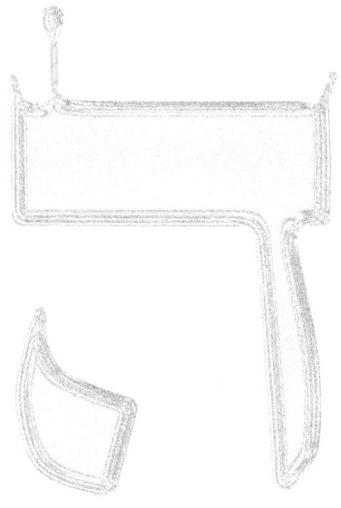

The Priesthood of Zion
Melchizedek's Order

5

The Priesthood of Zion
Melchizedek's Order

I have greatly deliberated, feeling the weight of what should and should not be said at the beginning of this section. I have written over and over, and scrapped it every single time because it leaned too heavily on what I thought would be best for you to hear about Melchizedek and His Priesthood; what I thought would be important points of clarification, demarcation, quantifiable revelation. But, ultimately that isn't what this is about. It's not what the order of Melchizedek is about.

I choose to walk in a very specific way in regards to Melchizedek and the order of Melchizedek. I hold it sacred. I won't play games or trade what is sacred on any trading floor. I will only stand here, with my heart as an offering in friendship with all of Heaven and say, I deeply love the heart of Melchizedek, and I am deeply committed to this beautiful priesthood rising. I am committed to helping them make the difficult choices necessary to walk in all they were born for, committed to equipping and empowering them to move forward and walk out their scrolls with all I have in my heart to give. I do not broach this subject outside of absolute reverence and awe of Yahweh. I do not assert any authority other than what I have chosen to do here:

To honor the Order of Melchizedek.
To honor my friendship with Melchizedek.
To honor my King, the King of the Universe.

To lead with my heart, knowing that you, the priesthood of Zion, can hear that frequency from anywhere in the world, and can perceive it through any noise that may assume to rise up and be heard over what is true and holy. The frequency of truth, of purity, cuts through what is trending and seemingly glamorous to stand authentically in all holiness and power.

I offer these poems to you as sacrifices, joys, and lessons of my own personal journey in hopes that you would, perhaps, know you're not alone if you stand in this Priesthood; In hopes that, if you are here and you have not heard the whistle of awakening, that your heart would hear it here.

You see, the Priesthood of Zion is a priesthood of the heart. That is the totality of these kings and priests, and that is their power. The power of a pure heart. There is no other way for them. Others may build with intellect and mental ascent, spiritual codes and formulas. The Order of Melchizedek lives, leads, builds with one thing: the highest, and most powerful piece of technology ever created- the human heart. They live with clean hands and a pure heart. They live contrary to the systems of the world. They live contrary to man-made religious systems. The Order of Melchizedek cannot be faked because the power of a pure heart cannot be faked. They don't seek attention, and they don't seek a platform. They live the power of being. They are honest, authentic, and feel no need to prove themselves. They don't just talk, they do, they *are*.

So, in this collections of poems, my greatest desire is that you would come home. Remember who you are. Return to your heart, for from it flows every kind of life, and in it resides the King of the Universe and all of heaven with Him. Kings and Priests of the Most High God, it's time to come home and stand up into who you were born to be.

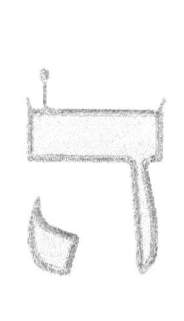

Priest

The priest
Who stands
With innocent hands
And makes a home
In the gleaming purity
Of a heart
Lodged immovable
In the heights
Of Zion
Will live forever
In the City of Gold

The Priest
Who endures
Softness of heart
And abides within
Rhythmic wings
Is sustained
In strength
Whispered
Upon songs
Of the wind

Who will ascend?

וקֹוֵי יהוה

Ve'koyei Yehovah - They who wait on the Lord

Let there be light and let there be light. This is the literal translation of Genesis 1:3. It isn't "Let there be light and there was light". It isn't a linear cause and effect. It's circular and unbroken, expressing the eternal perpetuity and never ceasing expansion of light. The Hebraic way is infinitely circular.

Command the Morning

I learn
to command the morning
listening to the sunrise song
of birds

I hold
command of the morning
standing righteous
in the light

I know
to sing the sun up from its rest
with eternal breath
in concentric circles

I've learned
to live in the house of unbroken hope
The light of Zion
forever rising from my voice

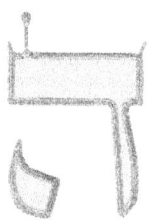

Taught

I am taught
In friendship
On the heights
Of Zion great

The secrets
Of friendship
Are the sacred
Treasure
Of kings and priests

The safety
Of a trustworthy
Heart
Is the promise
Of a steadfast
Life
Unwavering
In purity
Unmatched
In fulfillment

Friendship
Is
The crown
Of heaven
On
The head
Of the pure
In heart

When birds sing just before the light of dawn breaks, it's called the dawn chorus. It is said that birds who have larger eyes or who perch higher sing first because they perceive the light before others. This morning chorus happens all over the world every single day with the rising sun, but I've never heard a dawn song quite like the one in Jerusalem every morning. It's louder, it's sweeter, it's bolder, it's earlier. There is a quality to it that I've not heard any other place I've traveled in the world. Perhaps the birds in Jerusalem inherently know the heights of heaven, and that's why their song starts longer before the break of day.

There is something so sacred about the break of day, something arrestingly powerful about the emergence of fire and light upon the face of the morning. There is a tangible and distinct glory/weight in the literal and figurative morning. The priesthood of Zion has a special connection to the break of dawn, whether spiritual or in the natural. Some may find that they love the sunrise and always want to be awake for it. They want to feel that rush of the break of dawn, the overwhelming beauty and glory of a brand new day that bears just a slight likeness to the ultimate break of dawn when the Son returns in bodily form on the earth and the Lamb will be our light. We are wired for that day as kings and priests of Zion!

Dawn Song

The sacred song
Of the breaking dawn
Is a garment of light
For the priest who stands
In golden abundance

And like the melody
Of Jerusalem doves
We who sing
Bear the power
Of unshakable glory

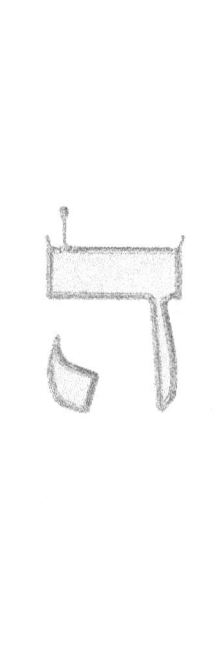

א

Fire of Zion

The ancients
Fixed
Zion in their gaze
With every breath
Immovable from
Her eternal radiance

The undying hope
Of the faithful
The surety
Of the righteous
Worth all
Our lives could offer

And we today
With Zion in our eyes
Know the power
Of eternal heritage
The living miracle
Of generational fire

So we hold the
Sacred fire now
To carry the city of God
To sing the songs
Of Zion

I learn what I know

I learn what I know
In the rising sun
In ancient paths
In the house of light
That holds the mysteries

        I learn what I know

I sit with the unseen
Understanding the voice

In the glow of Zion
I walk

I learn what I know
In stories kept hidden
In silent songs
In stones of righteousness
That stand and speak truth

        I learn what I know

I become what I know
A keeper eternal
Of the beauty of Zion
And her light forever

I wrote this poem after a heavenly encounter in which I was told, "You must learn what you already know. You must understand what you already know." Those words made me feel this truth in a way that changed my life forever. "Learn what you already know". In other words, perceive, understand, and commit to learn that which already resides in you and that which your heart already knows. He set eternity in our hearts, and He chose to dwell in our hearts. We know much more than we are consciously aware of. It's time to remember. Remember who you are, remember what you know. The depths of the riches of heaven, of Zion, of the heart of Yahweh, of His universe; It's all in our hearts. We know it, but we're not consciously aware. We must learn what we know.

Torah is

Torah is a fire
A hedge of separation

Torah, the protection
The voice of a mother
To cover and comfort

Torah is softness
And indomitable strength

Her might stands
She upholds all she bears
In unmovable confidence

She shields her children
And seals them
In everlasting surety

והאר עינינו בתורתך

וְהָאֵר עֵינֵינוּ בְּתוֹרָתֶךָ

V'har Eineinu b'Torahtecha translates to "And open our eyes to your Torah". Anytime you see the word "law" in the English translation of scripture, it is not from the Hebrew word law. It is the word Torah. If we open our hearts and eyes to the truth of Torah, we begin to understand the truth. Torah is the loving instructions of a good Father (A description I heard from Dr. Yana Sanders). The believing world has grossly misunderstood Torah. If we see Torah for what it truly is, we come to know that our Father has given us the best gift. The desire of His heart for us is to live an abundant, healthy, free, joyful life and He has provided instructions for us on exactly how to live the most optimal life on this earth. I deeply love Torah. I have since I was a child, and it has been a comfort, safety, wisdom, and source of nurture for my entire life. Still this prayer rings in my heart: *V'har Eineinu b'Torahtecha.*

Torah

Tongue could hardly tell
What Torah taught me

How it sang to me as a child
How before I knew its name
It knew me

The voice of love
My mother
Has pulled me
Into
Truth

Honey pours over me
In every letter
Alive with light

Running down my head
With shimmering oil

All my life
This song
Has held me
Tight
Secure

Zion holds the mysteries
And secrets of Love's utterance
Deep and high in mountain air
Whispers of ancient light
Breathe to be treasured

Deep grace

The face
Of the deep

These words

תורה רוח

Torah Ruach
Ruach- the word for breath, wind, spirit in Hebrew

Clean

A heart not hungry for power
But standing in surety

Lips not clamoring to speak
Yet opening in torrents of wisdom

Like water...

Clean.

Like pollen...

Clean.

Like breath...

Clean.

Like quiet...

Clean.

Purity is
the home
of power
And
the security
of the Righteous

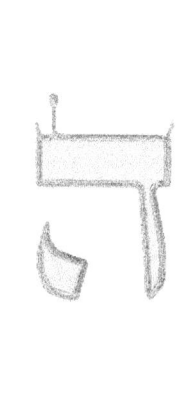

Weight and Glory

Weight of glory
Is carried
By the strength of love

We'll never know
The fullness of the
Brightness of majesty
Until we know
The depths of the
Brilliance of love

In open hands
Of tenderness
Love teaches us
The way of glory

In the gentle voice
Of belonging
Love teaches us
How to live

In never ceasing
Faithfulness
Of the height and length
Of love
We can learn to live
What we already know

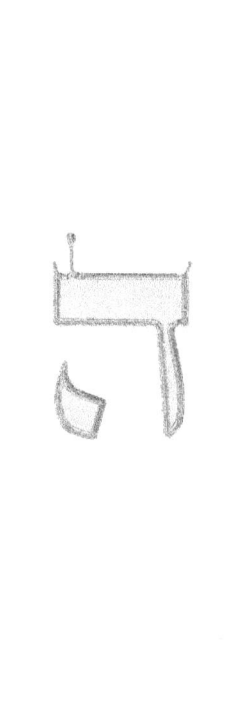

Nobility

Nobility
is at home
in humility

It finds
safety
in greatness
there

Noble hands
Build
Hold
Lift
Carry
Every good thing

Humility
Is abiding
strength,
focus,
perseverance
which enables
the noble heart
to stand
in power
and towering
Righteousness

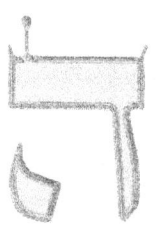

Priests of Abundance

I stand on the earth
From high above
Calling forth it's riches
From every corner
And hidden place

Now light churns up
The deep
In every color
In all brightness
The secret treasure
Breathes again
For the everlasting
Glory of Zion

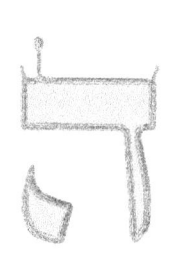

Tears of Priests : א

Tears of pain
Tears of sacrifice
Tears of compassion
Tears of grief
Tears of love
Tears of relief

These are
The wordless
Carriers
Of heaven
Given to earth
From holy hearts

Seeds
Sown into
Tangible
And
Intangible realms
From the unseen
Tumbling ground
Of purity

Tears of Priests : ב

When the tears
Of a priest fall

It shakes
The ground
With a power
Only tenderness
Can render

The seas know
The eternal song
Of their salty counterpart
Small drops
Running together
With all consuming mass
In alchemy
So great
Separateness
Doesn't
Exist

Every living thing
Stands
In awe
Holds
Their breath
Sings along

Creation
Turns
In reverence

The hands
Of the universe

Quiet the noise

The trees
Understand
Power
Falling from
Softness

There's a gasp
Open hands
Cavernous heart
A sweep of relief
Holy reverence

The universe
Bows
For the tears
Of a priest

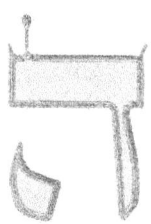

Lend Your Voice

Lend your voice
To the rising of the sun

And to the crowning
Of the morning
Sing the songs of Zion

Golden is the gate
Which holds the key
To the breaking day

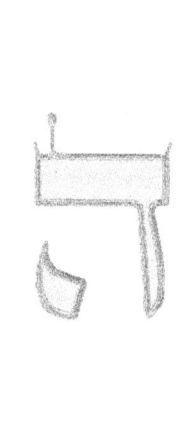

Unassuming Priests

Listen for mysteries revealed
in the voices of the ones
who sing
without demanding
your attention

Knowing that the
heart of first light
rests in the songs of birds
who sing
regardless
of who is listening

The power
of their melody
pulls the sun up
from the circle of
the deep

And every created thing
wakes
to the miraculous ordinary
of their dawn song

I stand as a priest
taught by the birds

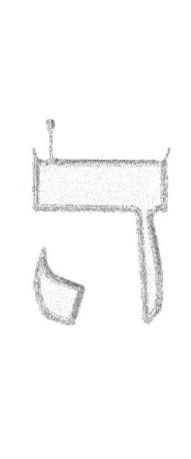

The Path of Love

Love is honest and simple
but the sacrifice
for its purity
is great

Only those who understand
its power and worth
will choose
to walk the path
on which
only love has a voice
that reaches
the heart

The path
on which love
is kept to its
inherent purity
is for the courageous

few will tread there

The cost of love
cannot be
overstated

Neither its simplicity
denied

What Matters to a Priest

My heart is the masterpiece
Of my life

The music of me
Playing all things
Pure and beautiful

The clear, clean
Breath
Of my heart
Standing in wisdom
Is the wind
Over the waters
Of making

I hold
Quiet
Unbroken
Communion
With all creation

I do not seek
To be known
By all
Nor stand before
Crowds

I do not derive value
From others
Hanging on my words
To know
What I know

My heart is the masterpiece

Of my life

I dwell in riches
Of eternity
A temple
Of grandeur
Am I
Inside

I do not want
Or need
Temporary fame

My hands hold
Keys
And my reward
Is alive in me

A letter to the Order of Melchizedek : Part 1

You must know
That your laughter
And your tears
Create
Things unseen
The power of your heart
Is what makes you different
From all the rest
Be comfortable with your very strong
Emotions
Be faithful to steward them, listen to them,
Let them be everything they were created to
Be for the glory of Zion
Never be ashamed of their power
You were uniquely created to carry the
Depth of their capacity into the earth

Learn to wield them for beauty, truth, and glory

You are more anchored to heaven
Than you are to the earth
Because of that
Creation loves you
And it will listen
Because you know and understand heaven
You have the unique ability to love creation
In a way no one else can

Realize that

Realize the strength of that
Realize the power of that
Realize the glory of that
But also realize

Because of your function
Few will understand
Few will truly see you for all you are
You must be not only anchored
To the ways of heaven
But to the heart of the Father for you
And you must be fully satisfied with your reward
Which is the Lord Himself

You have been uniquely created
To partner with righteousness and justice
Forever having loving-kindness and truth before you
To make manifest all the goodness of God in the earth
To make the crooked straight
And to establish on the earth
A resonant frequency of Zion,
Of the new Jerusalem, of the King you love

Be strong, be very courageous
And stand in the counsel of the Lord
All the days of your life
Revel in His justice and know that you
Are made to carry the weight of glory and
Strength of that justice into the earth

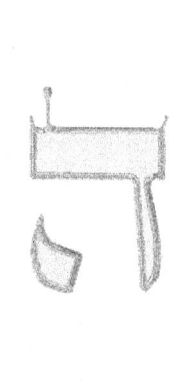

Judge

It is the tenderest
of hearts
which is most fit
to render righteous judgment

Beit HaMikdash (The Holy House/Temple)

Inaugurate
Stand
in what you have reclaimed

Breathe
in the holiness
of a pure altar

Fashion
with Wisdom
continually
the vessel
of light

You are the holy house

A Study in Tenderness

It matters...
the silent walk
in the woods
you took
that day

It matters...
your heart language
spoken to all
creation
yet heard
by no human ear

It matters...
that handful of earth
you held
to hear it weeping
and breathe
love back into
the torn

The silence
The song

The breath of life
The open hand

Most never perceive
their utmost
importance

You are rich
when you see
the gold

in the power
of a tender
heart

If the world
chooses
to accuse,
to make unfounded
assumptions
about,
to discard,
to treat unjustly

Let me choose
a tender heart
in the midst
of all

I will not
match the hardness
of injustice

I will become softer

For the heart of
tenderness
holds
the fountain of strength

And I walk
with wildflowers
on mountain tops
in valleys lush

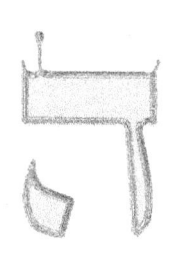

A letter to the Order of Melchizedek : Part 2

There are a great many people in this world who have had a life of extreme hardship, this is true. So in that way, you may not be unique, but very few have emerged with the kind of heart you have. That's what makes you different. It's not the difficulty or the trauma in and of itself, it's the choices you have made along the way to emerge with a soft and pure heart. That is the treasure of the priesthood of Zion.

Few have chosen the life of sacrifice that you have chosen. For some you've sacrificed marriage, for some, family, position, fame, monetary gain. You've sacrificed all that humanity counts as success and gain, comforts of earthly security and reward. You traded it all for the keeping of your heart. There are so very few who have truly chosen to walk this path because it is not easy. But we have known beauty in the midst of pain. We have learned that joy and sorrow can be two walls of the same house, and that justice prevails for the righteous.

In many ways it is a life of hiddenness. In that hiddenness lies a world that seems upside down to most, yet for us it is the place where all is right. Do not question, and do not move from the voice of Zion inside of you in the midst of a world screaming and pulling at you in its attempt to make you conform to its systems and beliefs. The world would like nothing better than to shake you from your heavenly place of connection and the power of living from your heart and walking in the ways of Zion. Never break your gaze with the King of Zion, priests and kings. Live unapologetically free. Live absolutely sure of where you were born. Remember, return, and never depart from your origins. Stand in trust, like Mount Zion, unshakable through all generations. For the world in which you were born holds the eternal heart of Yahweh, and no inferior system or belief will ever measure up to the splendor, magnificence, radiance, and heart intelligence of Zion. Do not trade anything for that which your heart has learned in the secret places of your life with the King of the Universe.

Stand in confidence, in faith, in trust, and move forward in every step of your life sure of this: all the power, provision, abundance you will ever need lives in your heart. Live in constant trust, covenant, and exploration of your heart, for it holds eternity and every expression of life. Your royalty is carried in your humble and generous heart, a home for the King of Zion, and a treasure house of heaven.

You, priests and kings in the order of Melchizedek, are the ones who have chosen at every turn, with every betrayal, every trauma, in the face of abuse, with every difficulty, in every injustice, to live with clean hands and a pure heart. Though the world may not see you for who you are, though you may forgo recognition and fame, you are seen and loved by all of heaven; held in the highest of regards. For the songs that Zion sings live in you, and you are the hope of a new day dawning.

In all of this, and above all, remember that He keeps you, and that His blessing reigns over every breath, and every beat of your beautiful heart. Rise up, priests and kings, and stand in the light of His face forevermore for the glory of Zion eternal and the city of Light.

יְבָרֶכְךָ יהוה וְיִשְׁמְרֶךָ
יָאֵר יהוה פָּנָיו אֵלֶיךָ וִיחֻנֶּךָּ
יִשָּׂא יהוה פָּנָיו אֵלֶיךָ וְיָשֵׂם לְךָ שָׁלוֹם

Y'varechecha Adonai v'yish'm'recha.
Ya-er Adonai panav eilecha vichuneka.
Yisa Adonai panav eilecha. v'yaseim l'cha shalom

The Lord blesses you and He keeps you.
He makes His face shine upon you He is gracious to you.
The Lord lifts up His countenance upon you and gives you peace.

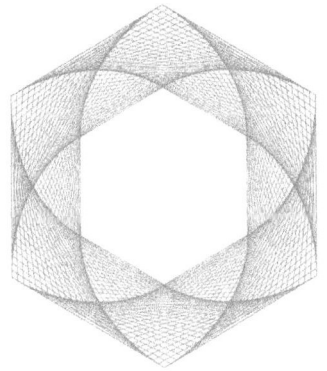

www.ingramcontent.com/pod-product-compliance
Lightning Source LLC
Chambersburg PA
CBHW032122090426
42743CB00007B/424